Reduce, Reuse, Recycle

Food

Alexandra Fix

Heinemann Library
Chicago, Illinois

Customer Service 888-454-2279
Visit our website at www.heinemannraintree.com

Designed by Steven Mead and Debbie Oatley
Printed in China by South China Printing Company Limited

12 11
10 9 8 7 6 5 4

ISBN 10-digit: 1-4034-9713-3 (hc) 1-4034-9721-4 (pb)

Library of Congress Cataloging-in-Publication Data
Fix, Alexandra, 1950-
   Food / Alexandra Fix.
      p. cm. -- (Reduce, reuse, recycle)
   Includes bibliographical references and index.
   ISBN 978-1-4034-9713-0 (hc) -- ISBN 978-1-4034-9721-5 (pb)
   1. Food industry and trade--Waste minimization--Juvenile literature. 2. Food conservation--Juvenile literature. 3. Food supply--Juvenile literature. 4. Recycling (Waste, etc.)--Juvenile literature. I. Title.
   TD899.F585F59 2007
   338.1'90286--dc22
                                2007002786

Acknowledgments
The author and publisher are grateful to the following for permission to reproduce copyright material: Alamy pp. **16** (Charles Stirling), **23** (Jim West), **27** (Graham Corney); Ardea pp. **7** (Jean Michel Labat), **8** (M. Watson), **18** (Chris Knights), **19** (John Cancalosi), **22** (John Daniels); Corbis pp. **4** (Paul Thompson), **5** (Patrick Giardino), **10** (Steve Miller/ Eye Ubiquitous), **11** (Chuck Savage), **12** (Theo Allofs/Zefa), **20** (Charles Gullung/Zefa), **25** (Royalty Free), **26** (Mika/Zefa); FLPA pp. **15** (Jim Brandenburg/Minden Pictures), **28** (Mike J. Thomas); Naturepl.com p. **9** (Lynn. M. Stone), Photolibrary.com pp. **6**, **13**, **14** (Jon Arnold Images), **17**, **21** (Workbook, Inc.), **24** (Botanica).

Cover photograph reproduced with permission of Corbis/Lois Ellen Frank.

Contents

Some words are shown in bold, **like this**. You can find out what they mean by looking in the glossary.

What Is Food Waste?

Food is wasted every day. Leftover food at restaurants is thrown out with the trash. In homes and stores, spoiled or outdated food often gets thrown out.

Food waste often ends up in the garbage.

↑ Taking more than you can eat creates food waste.

Food waste is food that is thrown away. One-half of the food that is grown in the United States goes to waste. If we buy and eat food more wisely, we can reduce food waste.

Why Do We Need Food?

Food has **nutrients** that help the body grow. Vegetables such as broccoli, carrots, and spinach have vitamins and minerals that keep the body healthy. Fruits, beans, nuts, grains, and dairy products are also important to a healthy diet.

A healthy diet includes lots of vegetables, fruits, and grains.

Being active is an important part of staying healthy.

Food gives the body **energy** to move. The body uses food as **fuel** so we can play sports and do other activities. The brain needs food to stay active, too.

Where Does Food Come From?

Most food is grown at large farms. Farmers grow crops such as vegetables, fruits, and grains. Some people have gardens and grow their own food.

This lettuce is ready to be picked for salads.

These dairy cows give us fresh milk.

Some farmers raise animals for meat and dairy products. Some fish are raised in special ponds called fish farms. Most fish are caught in oceans and rivers.

How Does Food Get to Our Homes?

These cans of beets are filled by a machine at a food processor plant.

After food crops are **harvested**, some food is taken to local farm stands or grocery stores. Many crops are shipped long distances to be sold in other states or countries.

Some of the crops go to a **food processor**. They are prepared and packaged. Food might be frozen or sealed in metal cans, glass jars, or plastic containers.

Many processed foods are sold at grocery stores.

11

How Can We Buy Food More Wisely?

Trucks and ships need gasoline to move food from place to place. Gasoline is made from oil, a **nonrenewable resource**. Once we use up the Earth's oil supply, it will be gone forever.

↑ Food may be shipped far from where it was grown.

Whenever you can, buy food grown near your **community**.

Buying food from local farmers wastes fewer nonrenewable resources. The food is moved only a short distance. This uses less gasoline.

Will We Always Have Food?

Food is a **renewable resource**. We can grow more food as we use it. In many places of the world, enough food is grown to feed everyone.

These fields of wheat are ready to be **harvested**.

Poor soil and bad weather make it difficult to grow food in some areas.

Some countries cannot grow the food they need. They may not be able to pay for food to be **imported** into their country. In some places, there are people who do not have enough money to buy food.

What Happens When We Waste Food?

Food that is not eaten becomes food waste. It is usually thrown out with other items in the trash. Food waste in trash attracts flies, rats, and other pests. These animals can spread diseases.

Trash buried in landfills can release a gas that is harmful to the **environment**.

Garbage trucks pick up household waste and bring it to **landfills**. Trash buried in landfills can **pollute** the soil and air.

When we waste food, more food has to be grown. It takes **fuel** to grow, process, and ship food. Most of the fuel to do this work comes from oil, a **nonrenewable resource**.

Large farm machines use fuel made from oil.

25% of the waste in here is PACKAGING! YOU can change this!

EX-CELL

CITY SERVI

These garbage trucks are dumping trash at a landfill.

Fuel is also used to bring food waste to **landfills**. The garbage truck runs on gasoline made from oil. If we reduce food waste, we will waste less fuel.

How Can We Reduce Food Waste?

You can reduce food waste at home or at school. Take only the food you can eat. Then eat what you have taken.

Store leftovers in containers that can be washed and reused.

Put leftovers in the refrigerator right away so they do not spoil. If you cannot finish a restaurant meal, take your leftovers home.

Use leftover breadcrumbs to fill a bird feeder in your backyard.

You can reduce food waste by using all the food you cook. Leftover chicken can be used in a soup. Water used to cook vegetables can also be added to soups.

Restaurants and grocery stores often give extra food to pantries. These are places that collect food for people who need it. You can bring food to pantries, too.

Many **community** groups collect canned goods for those in need.

How Can We Recycle Food Waste?

Leftover food that cannot be used again can be **recycled**. It can be broken down and changed into **compost**. Compost is made from food scraps and plant waste.

Compost adds **nutrients** to soil that help plants stay healthy.

Compost eventually turns into a brown, rich soil.

The scraps and waste are mixed together in a pile that is usually kept outside. Over time, these break down and create a natural **fertilizer**. Fertilizer is mixed with soil to help plants grow.

How Can You Take Action?

You can help reduce food waste. Ask family and friends to be more careful about wasting food. Use leftovers to make a new meal.

Take only as much food as you can eat.

You can add food scraps to a compost container every day.

At home, ask your family to start a **compost** pile to **recycle** food waste. Collect kitchen scraps and yard waste to add to the compost pile. If we reduce our own food waste, we can help keep our planet clean.

Make a Compost Pile

Ask an adult to help you with this project.

You can begin a simple **compost** pile.

1. Make a small pile of dried leaves and add dirt. Add equal amounts of green and brown materials (see page 29).

2. Turn the pile with a shovel or pitchfork at least once a week.
3. Add a little water if the pile gets too dry.

After several months, the mixture will begin to break down into a dark, rich compost that can be added to your garden or yard.

Green (wet) materials include:
grass clippings, old flowers, weeds, and kitchen scraps like egg shells, vegetable or fruit peelings, coffee grounds, and tea bags.

Brown (dry) materials include:
dead leaves, straw, wood chips, old potting soil, and shredded newspaper.

Glossary

community	group of people who live in one area
compost	food scraps and plant waste that can be added to soil
energy	power to do work
environment	natural surroundings for people, animals, and plants
fertilizer	substance added to the soil to help plants grow
food processor	place where food is prepared, canned, and packaged
fuel	something that is burned for power or heat
harvest	picking crops when they are ready to eat
import	bring goods into one country from another country
landfill	large area where trash is dumped, crushed, and covered with soil
nonrenewable resource	material of the earth that cannot be replaced by nature
nutrient	substance in food that keeps the body healthy and helps it grow
pollute	harm the air, soil, or water with chemicals or wastes
recycle	break down a material and use it again to make a new product
renewable resource	something that can be replaced by nature

Find Out More

Books to Read

Galko, Francine. *Earth Friends at the Grocery Store*. Chicago: Heinemann Library, 2004.

Inskipp, Carol. *Reducing and Recycling Waste*. Milwaukee: Gareth Stevens, 2005.

Spilsbury, Louise. *Why Should I Eat This Carrot?* Chicago: Heinemann Library, 2003.

Web Sites

The Environmental Protection Agency works to protect the air, water, and land. The organization has a special Web site for students at www.epa.gov/kids.

Earth911 is an organization that gives information about where you can recycle in your community. Their Web site for students is http://www.earth911.org/master.asp?s=kids&a=kids/kids.asp.

Index